Obtaining a Firearms License (FFL) in the USA

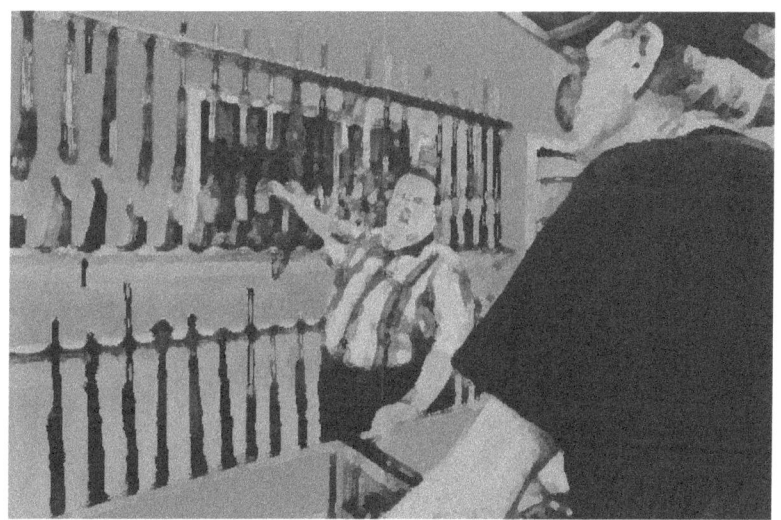

This mini guide is proudly brought to you by:

Lazaros Georgoulas
Researcher and Author
lazageo@gmail.com

To get your FFL Kit, click:
http://firearmslicense.webs.com/

ISBN-13: 978-1499321791

ISBN-10: 1499321791

Printed by CreateSpace, An Amazon.com company

Introduction

Becoming a Federal Firearms Licensee (FFL) in the US is not at all an expensive or complex procedure. But there are certain steps and rules that should be followed in order to have your license accepted as soon as possible by the United States Department of Justice. The cost to file an FFL application (Type 1 Dealer) is around $200 for the first 3 years (at the time of writing this). After that it is much cheaper!

You must wait at least 6-7 weeks before your application is reviewed and processed by the ATF (Bureau of [**A**]lcohol,

[**T**]obacco, [**F**]irearms and Explosives)

Before everything else you must decide that this business is for you. If you always had a passion for guns and ammo and if you have the spirit of the Merchant inside you then here's how to do it. The process works as described below:

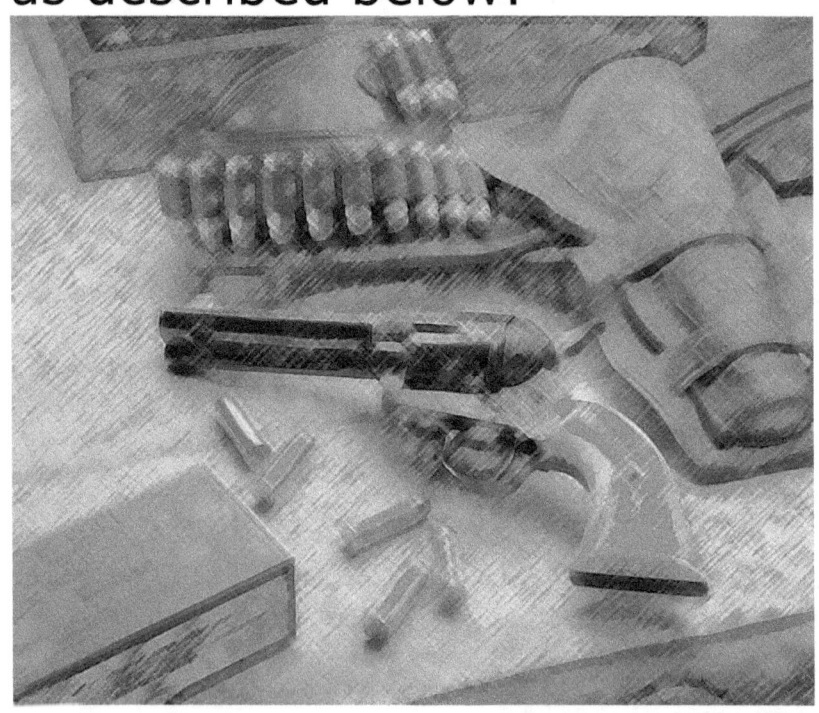

Step 1:

First you must file your application, also called "FFL" to the ATF. The perfectly completed application should be send to the ATF post office box listed in the application form. You must also pay an application fee either by credit card, check, money order and not cash.

Step 2:

Your application will be processed within 6-7 weeks and only after the application fee has been payed. Then your FFL application will be included in the ATF's database and a full review will be commenced. Review includes fingerprint clarity inspection, background check as required by law etc. Then the ATF will define a "Sole Proprietor" who is the actual firearms business manager or owner (you).

Step 3:

Then your FFL application will be send to the nearest ATF field office that is responsible for your area (where business will be conducted). The ATF office supervisor will assign an investigator to you, also known as IOI (Industry Operations Investigator). This person will interview you regarding State, Federal and Local requirements. The IOI will proof-read your FFL application making sure everything is in place.

Step 4:
The IOI will prepare a full review of your idea/project to buy and sell firearms along with

their opinion of whether your FFL application should be accepted or denied. It is a fact that if the IOI recommends that you should be accepted as a gun merchant then you will be accepted. But you must also get a recommendation from the ATF field office supervisor who will also review your FFL.

Step 5:

If all the requirements are met, then your application will be accepted and stored. Then you will be issued your firearms license and you are ready to buy and sell guns.

To avoid denial make sure your application is perfectly completed, that you comply with all Local and State laws and that you and the persons involved in the business have never willfuly violated the "Gun Control Act" (the ATF will do strict background check).

If successful, you must have a business plan, a list of gun wholesalers, an after-sales support system. And then you can start the firearms business. You know that when people buy a gun they will always need ammo so you know you can have returning customers. The more professional and experienced you appear to your buyers, the more returning customers you will have.

Then, there are many other issues that you will need to consider as you learn the nust and bolts of the firearms industry. Things like full copies of all laws governing guns as you will encounter various scenarios as an FFL Holder, a way to keep detailed records of every single firearm transaction (as required by law) etc.

If you are interested in the firearms business and you need more information about FFL then consider this Firearms License Kit:

http://hyperdeals.biz/go/11/

Important Notices

Let's see some important notices that you should consider before applying for gun merchant and file your FFL application:

1. First of all you must intend to start a firearms business before applying. The ATF officers will easily identify whether you truly want to engage to this business or not.

2. After you send your application, an ATF officer will contact you so you better watch for their call. It is important to get a good recommendation from them.

3. While in business, every single firearms transaction must be recorded and you are responsible for the integrity of the records (required by law).

4. The ATF has the right to access your transaction records (required by law)

5. The ATF will notify other authorities about your FFL application.

6. USA States might have certain laws that require extra licenses or/and permits to obtain an FFL. You must always have a good knowledge of the State laws governing the firearms industry.

7. You should consider other firearms business requirements as required by State laws. For example collection of sales taxes, zoning restrictions, cash bonds, liability insurance etc. Also, that you will be required to provide genuine fingerprints

and pay an application fee to the ATF.

Are you are interested in the firearms business? Do you want to become an FFL Holder? Then consider this Firearms License Kit:

http://hyperdeals.biz/go/11/

This Kit has helped thousands of individuals to become licensed firearms dealers and earn a lot of $$$.

Common Questions

Here are some answers to common questions that you might have before sending your FFL application to ATF:

Question: How long does it take for ATF to review and process your firearms license application?

Answer: The ATF must approve or disapprove your application within 2 months from the day they receive your application

Question: If I want to renew or modify my FFL, what is the process?

Answer: These applications are different than the initial FFL license application. They are directed to a specific department/office. Depending on the uniqueness of each case, review processes vary. But if the firearms merchant makes sure all requirements are met and guarantees compliance with all State or Local laws (among other requirements), then the ATF will quickly renew the FFL.

Question: When do I get the actual FFL in my hands?

Answer: After the ATF receives your application they first check if it is properly completed and if all the required info is written there. You must also pay an application fee before they process your application (payable via credit card, check or money order. No cash). FFL licenses are generated on business days and are sent first class mail to the address you provide in your firearms application.

Question: In what cases may the ATF delay the acceptance of my application?

Answer: The ATF mentions that the majority of people who file their FFL applications cannot be easily contacted by the ATF officers so as to schedule an interview (required by law). If you want to avoid your FFL review being delayed then keep an eye for their call. Other reasons for delay is when the FBI cannot perform a complete background check due to fingerprints that could not be identified. In this case you might be asked to re-submit your firearms license application.

Question: Do I need to keep records for every single firearm sale? What are the ATF requirements?

Answer: All FFL Holders (Licensees) are required by law to maintain records for every firearm transaction. Each record should include all required details about the purchaser (e.g. name, address, age etc.)

Do you want your FFL application to be reviewed quickly and become accepted?

Then make sure it is perfectly completed, that you have paid the fee to the ATF and that you provided them with fresh fingerprints in the fingerprint card. And of course, never file such an application if you or anyone involved in the gun business have violated the "Gun Control Act".

If you don't have a clue on how to prepare your application, how to send it or how to acquire the FFL license and start your new firearms business then consider this Firearms License Kit:

http://hyperdeals.biz/go/11/

This Kit has all you need to apply for a firearms dealer. It is for those who see this business seriously.

THE END

Hope you enjoyed this mini intro-book!

If you have it in you, then begin thinking about your future business selling guns.

Good luck and may you succeed in your goals.

Serious FFL Kit:
http://firearmslicense.webs.com/

www.ingramcontent.com/pod-product-compliance
Lightning Source LLC
Chambersburg PA
CBHW070737180526
45167CB00004B/1788